High Frequency Living for Starseeds

Starseeds

The Art of Eating, Living, and Awakening as a Starseed on Earth.

CHELSEA YERGENSEN

1

Published by Know By Soul Publishing

First edition, 2025
Printed with love in the United States of America
ISBN: ISBN:979-8-9994111-2-9 (paperback)
Published by: Know By Soul Publishing
@knowbysoul
Cover and interior design by Chelsea Yergensen
Created in partnership with Spirit, Earth, and the unseen realms
Designed with Canva
For blessings, permissions, or speaking requests:
knowyoursoul.yogi@gmail.com

Dedication

To my husband, Erik—thank you for always supporting me on this spiritual path, even when you don't totally know what I'm talking about. Your grounded presence anchors me.

To my son, my indigo flame—your wild, rebellious spirit pushes me to grow every single day.

To my daughter, my crystal light—thank you for holding space for all of us, radiating peace, wisdom, and unconditional love.

And for every soul walking through the fire—may you remember who you are.

TABLE OF CONTENTS

Part 3: Nourishment for the Starseed Body

Please know—I don't write this book as someone who has it all figured out.

I write it as someone who has walked through the fire.

Through addiction.

Through mental illness, anxiety, and depression.

Through suicidal ideation.

Through the deep wounds of sexual abuse.

What saved me wasn't one thing. It was many:

My husband, Erik.

My children.

Meditation.

Yoga.

Real food.

Mindful, intentional living.

A will to persevere. And above all—a deep faith in something greater than me.

A trust that the Universe will always provide, and always protect me, even when I couldn't see the way forward.

This book isn't about perfection.

It's about possibility.

It's about remembering who you are, reclaiming your wholeness, and nourishing your body and life from the inside out.

I honor the wisdom of many cultures, but this book is simply my story, shaped by my own experience with the modern American diet and way of life.

Wherever you are on your path, this book is for you.

With love and light, Chelsea

Part One

The Frequency Within

Chapter 1: We are Frequency

You are not just a body. You are not just the physical shell that holds your organs.

You are pure light. You are stardust.

This is something we've forgotten in our day-to-day lives. With so many distractions, demands, and decisions, there is little space left to remember our true essence.

This book is here to help you remember who you are.

You are frequency.
You are vibration in motion.

But what does that really mean?
It means you are the sum of your choices.
You hold the frequency of your food, your music, your clothing, your viewing habits, your actions, your inactions, your thoughts, and the company you keep—family, friends, peers.
So I ask you:
What did you choose today? What vibration are you holding right now?
Because this is no small thing. It's a powerful responsibility. Our choices are our karma in motion. *Instead of blaming, complaining, or shaming—what would happen if we chose to take full responsibility for every single thing in our lives? Everything that happens to us, around us, and within us? That level of ownership is where transformation begins.*

For generations, the human body has adapted to its environment. But today, the environment is shifting. Our food is shifting. We are shifting. The human body is evolving.

For decades, we've used food not as nourishment—but as numbing. As a distraction. As poison, if I dare say. But we can no longer function—let alone thrive—if we continue down the same path.

The frequencies on Earth are rising. Our bodies are rising with it. And our food, thoughts, beliefs, and daily habits must rise too.

As Starseeds, we can no longer digest what dims our light. We are moving toward crystalline bodies—light bodies—ones that must be fed with aligned, conscious foods.

This book is a beginning. A remembering. A prayer.

High-Frequency Foods for Starseeds is your first step in reclaiming your starseed lineage.

For generations, waves of Starseeds have arrived on Earth:

- Those who came to shake up old systems
- Those who hold calm amidst chaos
- And those who came to heal and anchor the new light streaming into the planet

What Is a Starseed?

A Starseed is believed to be a soul originating from higher realms or other dimensions, incarnated on Earth to assist in the planet's spiritual evolution. These individuals often feel a strong sense of purpose and a longing for a world that aligns with their inner wisdom.

Indigo Children are considered a specific group of Starseeds. The term was popularized in the 1990s by Lee Carroll and Jan Tober in their book The Indigo Children: The New Kids Have Arrived. They describe Indigo Children as possessing "unique psychological attributes, such as heightened intuition, a strong sense of purpose, and a tendency to challenge authority and traditional systems.

These children are thought to be here to break down outdated structures and pave the way for a more enlightened society."

Dolores Cannon's book The Three Waves of Volunteers and the New Earth describes three distinct waves of Starseeds—souls who came to Earth with a mission to assist in humanity's evolution.

The first wave came between the 1940s and 1960s. The second wave followed in the 1960s through the 1980s. The third wave began in the 1990s and continues today.

In this book, I'm focusing mostly on the more recent arrivals— those often referred to as Indigo, Crystal, and Rainbow children. These are the highly sensitive, intuitive beings who came in already coded for this time. Many of them are our children... and some of us were just early.

My Experience as a Starseed

As a Starseed, I've often felt like I didn't quite belong here. This world—so loud, so harsh, so fast—has always felt a little off to me. I'm highly sensitive, especially to sound and energy, and for most of my childhood, I quietly wondered, What's the point of all this? Why am I here? I didn't always fit in, so I learned to conform just to get by. I muted my sensitivity. I numbed my discomfort.

For years, that meant turning to alcohol and drugs—coping mechanisms that dulled the parts of me that actually needed the most care. It wasn't until I began to remember who I really am, and truly nourish my Starseed nature, that things started to shift.

I stopped running. I started listening. And everything changed.

As Earth herself evolves, the children arriving now hold new codes—new frequencies. They are highly sensitive to everything: food, energy, vibration. I am one of those Starseeds, from the 80's Indigo wave. And my children are too. My son in particular—so sensitive, so radiant—is the inspiration for this book. Our journey together has been intense and beautiful. Full of challenges, full of breakthroughs, and full of sacred nourishment.

This is not just another cookbook. This is a transmission from one mother to another. From one loving soul to anyone in a role of nurturing the next generation.

This book is for those who feel the call to raise the frequency of the planet through the kitchen, through connection, and through love.
It is for the awakening souls—new and seasoned—who are looking for practical guidance and spiritual remembrance.

Inside these pages, you'll find recipes, invocations, real life stories, and even a little humor.

You'll find pieces of our journey, and reminders to support the ones you love the most.

Welcome home.
Let's nourish the light together.

Chapter 2: The Starseed body

A Starseed body is one that regulates on vibration. A body that can no longer pretend. When a Starseed body is out of alignment, there is no hiding from yourself. You may notice signs. Whispers. Warnings.

These are some common signals your Starseed body—your light body—is unhappy with your current vibrational choices:

- Low energy
- Feeling heavy or weighed down
- Difficulty staying present
- Brain fog
- Depression
- Anxiety
- Weight gain
- Mood swings
- Constipation
- Digestive issues
- Adrenal burnout
- Poor sleep
- Cravings
- Lack of synchronicities
- Emotional overwhelm from simple tasks
- Eczema and other skin imbalances

These are not random. These are signals. I see them in my own home, and in the homes of those I love. When we eat out of alignment with our energetic bodies, our physical bodies suffer. But this is not a punishment—it is a blessing. A lesson. Our bodies are no longer allowing us to sit in numbness. Yes, breaking free of old patterns is hard. But isn't your well-being, your clarity, your frequency, more important?

As Starseeds, our bodies are sensitive, intuitive, and multidimensional. Putting foods into these sacred vessels that do not align with our higher vibration will no longer suffice.

Low-Vibration Foods

What lowers the light of the Starseed body?
- Highly processed foods
- Refined sugar (white, brown & powdered sugar, dextrose, sucrose, glucose, high fructose corn syrup)
- Gluten
- Conventional dairy
- Alcohol
- Factory farmed meats
- Foods void of life force
- Seed oils (particularly when heated)
- Farmed fish
- Chemically treated oats
- Conventional corn

These foods may be common, but they are not neutral. They carry a frequency—of suffering, of stagnation, of disconnection.

Feed the Light Within

You are not just feeding a body—you are fueling a frequency. Here are some options that support the light body:
- Whole, real minimally processed foods
- Seasonal, local veggies and fruits (when available)
- Organic ingredients when accessible (look into clean fifteen and dirty dozen lists)
- Meats raised with humane, respectful standards
- High quality raw dairy (if consumed)
- Organic oats
- Nuts, seeds, legumes, quinoa, rice
- Foods with few ingredients
- Homemade meals made with intention

There is no shame in where you are now. We are all learning. One meal at a time. One snack at a time. One choice at a time. These shifts aren't always easy. But the support on the other side is immense. Eventually, eating real food—alive food—will be the norm again. Until then, we walk the path of remembering.

Starseed Children Feel Everything

A gentle reminder: young Starseeds feel the vibration of what they eat. They don't just digest food—they embody it. If your child (or inner child) experiences sudden emotional outbursts, behavior shifts, or nervous system dysregulation... it may not be "just a mood." It may be the food.

A Moment to Consider...

A cow, pig, or chicken is raised on a factory farm—no sunlight, no fresh water, no freedom. They are filled with hormones, antibiotics, fear, and sadness. Then, they are butchered in barbaric ways and sent into the food system.

Now, imagine a highly sensitive Starseed—of any age—consuming that frequency. Do you believe it affects their mind, body, and spirit? How could it not? We've been given antidepressants, prescriptions, and therapy to "fix" the symptoms. But what if—just what if—it starts with the food?

What if being conscious of what we place into our sacred vessels could shift the entire health of humanity? I don't know the answers to every question. I don't know your exact story. But I know mine. And I share that with you next.

Chapter 3: My Frequency Journey

"When you change your energy, you change your life."- Dr. Joe Dispenza

Where do I begin?

Do I begin by telling you that changing your frequency isn't just possible—it's divinely supported? That God, the universe, and your most masterful self are all aligned with your transformation? The energetic blueprint of the cosmos is inviting you—urging you—to shift. And to shift swiftly.

Do I start by sharing my lowest-frequency moment—blackout drunk on alcohol and benzodiazepines, waking up in jail? Nah... I'll save that for the second book.

Let's begin instead with my highest vibrational moments—and how I got there through food. The first time I ate kale, I was dating my now-husband. He shopped at Whole Foods and ate organic; I did none of these things. The first couple of times he cooked kale for me, I had the worst stomach aches of my life. I had to come up with excuses to leave his apartment just to run home and use the bathroom. My body simply wasn't capable of digesting that kind of high-frequency food yet.

Fast forward ten years—and kale is one of my favorite foods. I crisp it up in the oven, and even the kids love it now.

As a child, we ate broccoli, cauliflower, and other simple, home-cooked meals. Our diet was minimal but nourishing. But things shifted in college. That's when I began using food to numb out. I missed my family, my small hometown, and everything I knew.

San Francisco was exciting, but overwhelming—and it took a toll on my emotional body. That's when the overeating began. The low-vibration food matched how I was feeling inside. Lost, lonely, and disconnected.

"Everything you see in your outer world is a reflection of what's happening on the inside." Dr. Joe Dispenza. My internal frequency was low—and so was my outer world. My actions, my food, my habits, and my environment all mirrored that heaviness. I stayed in that space for nearly a decade.

But in the last ten years—and especially the last 18 months—I've made a complete 180. I stopped drinking alcohol in January 2024, and that's when my real life began. Before that, I was in my suffering era. I'm proud to say I'm now fully in my happiness era.

Over these past 18 months, I've been cleansing my body on a cellular level. My vessel is now able to hold higher frequency energy because I've released so many of the habits that kept me heavy.

Are they all gone? No way. Do I still snack or eat one too many slices of my own homemade bread? Yep. But I've made massive shifts. My body now refuses to accept what it once tolerated— ultra-processed foods, excess cane sugar, conventional dairy. I don't restrict—I listen.

Last year was one of the hardest of our lives. My husband and I both experienced what I can only describe as a full ascension— our bodies transitioning toward a more crystalline, light-based expression. It left us with no choice but to stop eating certain foods.

As I wrote in Chapter 1: we can no longer digest what dims our light. Our main symptom? Pain.

Excruciating pain when eating. Then came issues with the liver, gallbladder, lymphatic system, and adrenals.

After years of ignoring my body's subtle signals, she finally had to scream. And I listened. Now, I'm stepping into a new phase—one led by intuition. The very intuition that brought me here. That's guiding this book. That is guiding you, too. I trust that I will continue to make wise choices for my body, mind, and spirit.

Because here's what I know now: We create our reality. Everything within is reflected on the outside. Our bodies are always listening. She—your body—doesn't know the difference between you thinking the thing and actually doing the thing. Every thought we have sends a signal to our bodies. Let's become conscious of the thoughts, words, and stories we tell ourselves and those around us. Together, let's sing a song of blessing rather than burden. And that... leads us into the next chapter: how our thoughts and energy shape the food we prepare, bless, and receive.

Chapter 4: Thoughts, Blessings & Invocations

The Energy You Stir In

We've all heard the old saying: "The chef cries while cooking, and everyone who eats his food ends up crying too." Well—this isn't far from the truth of vibration. Food is alive. It's conscious. It absorbs the energy you imprint on it.

In this section, I want to share a few simple, mindful kitchen practices that bring spirit and intention back into the food we prepare.

Your energy is transferred to your food. So ask yourself: What energy do I want my loved ones consuming?

My husband loves to cook—and he's really good at it. He puts on music, moves slowly and intentionally, sings, dances, and somehow keeps six things going at once without stress. And the food? Every single dish is divine. He has a natural ability to uplift his food without even realizing it.

We're blessed to shop at a local farmer's market weekly, which of course contributes to the flavor and vitality of his meals. But honestly—it's the love he pours in that makes them what they are.

If You Can't Buy Local, Bless It Anyway

Not everyone has access to seasonal, organic, or local ingredients. That's okay. Energy is everything. You can bring your food into energetic alignment through prayer, mantra, visualization, or sound.

- Speak into or over the food
- Visualize golden light infusing it
- Align your breath and body with the vibration you want to create

One of my favorite food blessings is from a spiritual mentor, Pamela Aaralyn: "May a cosmic consciousness invigorate this food and elevate my form."

And a simple one from my son: "May this yummy and delicious food elevate my body and soul." It doesn't have to be complicated. It just has to be intentional.

Water Blessings

Water is amazing.

As my husband always says, "Water is life, my friend."

And truly—it is.

The quality of your water matters, and so do the blessings you speak over it. All of the blessings I've shared so far can be offered to your water too. Talk to it. Thank it. Blow golden light into it with your breath.

One of our favorite rituals is setting out a glass jar of water under the full moon. The moon supercharges the water with healing frequency and soft power. She helps us release what no longer serves. She takes our sorrow, our grief, our heaviness— and transmutes it. When you drink your moon water, let it be a sacred act.

A moment of remembrance that you are more than a body. You are energy. You are light. You are intention made real.

Believe the water is sacred—and it will be.

Believe the water is healing your wounds, fears, and worries— and it will.

Because it's not just water. It's consciousness in liquid form.

Blessing Beyond Food

On this path to wellness and alignment with our 5D health blueprint, I've extended these practices to everything—even vitamins and supplements.

I bless what I pour into smoothies or mix into drinks. And I've noticed… it matters. There was a time recently when I was going through a wave of sorrow, self-pity, and emotional heaviness. I realized I was preparing my son's supplements while sitting in that vibration. And you know what? I believe it caused a slight setback in his energy. Our intention carries a charge, even in the highest quality supplements.

We are far from our original design… But I believe we can return to the divine blueprint. Together, let's remember what it means to live in alignment with God's image of us.

A Quick Word on Supplements

I won't go too deep into the world of supplements here, but I will say this:

- Choose high-quality, third-party tested brands
- Avoid products full of fillers, binders, or hidden heavy metals
- Listen to your body and your intuition

Chapter 5: Cosmic Kids & Conscious Eating

So how do we get our children to eat food that's alive and full of life force?

We make it for them.

We eat it with them.

As we've transitioned from fake food to real, whole food in our home, the kids have come along beautifully. Was it hard at first? Yes—there were tears, fears, and some upset little humans. But fast forward a few months, and now we all eat the same meals together at dinner. My son even requests quinoa now—when, at first, he literally couldn't even keep it in his mouth. He said it felt "too weird." That's the thing: children's taste buds evolve. They adapt to what we feed them. Of course, they still ask for what other kids are eating—and we let them have it occasionally. But at home, and in their lunches, we stick with real, whole foods.

Start Slowly

Start by swapping one thing at a time.

If your family loves gluten, begin by reducing it gradually. A little less each day. A little less each week. Then phase it out of the house. Eventually, it becomes something you only eat on special occasions, if at all.

Still Drinking Cow's Milk?

If cow's milk has been part of your daily routine, consider exploring gentler alternatives. Try slowly shifting toward plant-based milks that support your body with lighter, higher-frequency nourishment. Raw cow's milk is in its own category, but it can still be inflammatory. We prefer organic coconut milk. Other options: almond milk, oat milk (check for no seed oils!). Always check labels. Even "clean" products can hide junk.

The Emotional Cheese Bond

This one's real. I get it—how will I live without cheese?
We now eat raw goat's milk cheese and the occasional sheep's cheese, but for a long time, we only ate cashew cheese—or none at all.
And honestly? Your body gets used to it. Eventually, it prefers less inflammation.

On Sweeteners

We use raw honey most often.
I bake with it, stir it into tea, and the kids even chew on honeycomb as a sweet treat (find it at your local honey supplier). We use maple syrup on occasion, but honey is our go-to.

Grains & Roots

We still eat rice—it's comforting, grounding, and for now, still aligned. We also eat quinoa, which is actually a seed, not a grain. It's gut-friendly, nourishing, and versatile. We've cut out white potatoes but still enjoy sweet potatoes—especially roasted or mashed with cinnamon. The kiddos love it. (A recipe is attached!)

Let's Talk Bread

This one's a process. If you tolerate high-quality sourdough made from wheat flour, that's a great place to start. If not, it may be time to try homemade gluten-free bread. (I've included recipes in the back of the book!) Or... you can order from me. I've been making gluten-free sourdough for almost two years, and it's a staple in our home.

Make It Fun
- Use cute cookie cutters to shape veggies or fruit
- Make the plate colorful and creative
- Let them help you stir, sprinkle, or bless the food

In a Dr. Joe Dispenza kids meditation, he says: "Tell yourself it's good for you—and it will taste good to you." We say this often —because it's true: Real food is good for you. Your body needs it. And beyond that—you create your reality. Your words shape your experience. So start by saying: Real food is good food. Even one intentional choice a day can shift everything.

Mindful Eating Matters

Where and how your kids eat matters too.

We're still unlearning our own habits—like mindlessly eating while watching TV. We've cut that way back. There are still some movie nights where we eat and watch, but they're rare. Creating healthy, high-frequency habits around food starts now.

A Note on Snacks

Our kids' favorite dessert right now? Frozen blueberries.

When we started this journey, it was rice crackers with peanut butter and bananas. We've moved away from that—at least for now. It might come back later, but not as a bedtime snack.

We also stopped eating peanut butter. Why? Because it's hard to know the quality or condition of peanuts before they get to us. If they've been cooked and reheated too many times, mold growth becomes an issue. When we began our family's healing journey last year we all had significant levels of mycotoxins (mold) in our bodies. Mold impacts your immune system as well as your organs. I believe it was from years of eating peanut butter and low quality grains.

Now we eat sunflower seed butter or almond butter occasionally. Sun butter was an acquired taste, but they've grown to love it.

I hope this chapter shows you that change is possible. If you've been curious about eating more intentionally—start small. Begin by eliminating the foods we're most addicted to (and most misaligned for Starseeds):

- Gluten

- Dairy

- Processed sugar

There are always better options.
Be a rebel. Go against the grain. Get creative.

Learn to love real food again. Your body and soul will thank you.

Chapter 6: From Numbing to Nourishment

As I shared earlier, I've been an emotional eater for about half of my life. It's a pattern I'm now mindfully choosing not to pass on to my children.

Through this journey, I've learned a lot—through struggle, through softness, and through grace. And from it, I've created some beautiful tips, recipes, and reflections to share. One thing that's helped me is asking myself a very honest question: "What am I really hungry for?"

If I've just eaten a full meal and I still find myself wanting more food, I pause. I ask myself—What do you need right now? What part of you is asking to be seen? And then I gently remind myself: Your stomach is full. You're not hungry for food.

On the good days, I'm able to sit with that awareness. I give it two or three minutes. I breathe. And almost always, the "craving" or that deep sense of emptiness starts to dissolve. On the other days, I give myself grace and choose the healthiest option I can. That's why I'm sharing two of my favorite "craving-filler" recipes—they've supported me when I needed something comforting but conscious.

Of course, not every craving is about food. Sometimes it's a hunger for peace. Sometimes it's connection. Sometimes it's grief, boredom, anxiety, loneliness, or simply the need to be held.

And for the cravings we've been numbing for years with drugs, alcohol, shopping, distractions ... those take time. They require gentle participation in your own healing. They ask for radical self-acceptance—and an enormous amount of compassion. That brings me to something I hold close: Forgiveness.

Forgiveness for the moments we didn't show up the way we wanted to. Forgiveness for the nights we numbed. Forgiveness for the days we forgot to nourish ourselves with love. Forgiving ourselves (and others) is liberating. It's not always easy—but it will always lead to the expansion of your soul.

So here's my best advice:
Do your best. Bless the rest.
Speak to yourself with kindness and compassion.
And walk this path with grace, one choice at a time.

Part Two

The Frequency Around Us

Why High Vibrational Living?

The point of high-vibrational living isn't to be perfect. It's to experience a more joyful, aligned, and vibrant time on Earth. We chose to come to Earth School. To learn the hard lessons, break ancestral patterns, release generational trauma, and to acquire self-mastery by releasing our attachments to suffering. Easy right?! NO WAY.
But the journey back to oneness doesn't have to be walked in pain. We don't have to live in sickness anymore. We can make conscious choices that raise our frequency, nourish our bodies, and return us to harmony.

Health is gold. Health is wealth.

Chapter 7: Your Home as Sanctuary

High-Vibrational Living in the Home

What we put on our bodies carries just as much frequency as what we put in them.

From laundry soap to lotion, dishwashing detergent to hand soap, deodorant to diapers—even our underwear—everything we use daily holds a vibration. The residue left behind from toxic products soaks into our skin and lingers in our energetic field. That laundry soap? It lives in your clothes. That hand soap? You absorb it multiple times a day.

One of the most toxic offenders in the modern home?
Fragrance.
Fragrances are often labeled harmless, but they are anything but. Synthetic scents are known to disrupt hormones, stress the nervous system, and impact your frequency field. Removing artificial fragrances is one of the most powerful and immediate changes you can make.

Begin shifting to clean beauty and body care. I'll list some of our favorite conscious brands at the end of this book.
This journey isn't about perfection—it's about lowering your toxic load, little by little.
It's choosing foods that are real, clothes that breathe, and products that don't poison your system. Remember: your vibration is the sum of your choices.
You don't have to overhaul everything overnight. Start slowly.
I began over eight years ago, and now it all feels second nature.
But at the start, it was overwhelming. The moment you pull back the curtain, *the matrix begins to crumble.*

You realize that nearly everything around us is designed to keep us distracted, disconnected, and unwell. It's a hard truth—but it's also your turning point.
You have a choice. You can live aligned, clean, healthy, and closer to God's original image of us.

One step at a time.

High-frequency life is a healthy life—and the more we align, the more we thrive.

A Note on Cleansing Your Space

I'm not a professional space clearer, but I'll share what's worked for me. Our homes hold energy—layers of it. From the everyday emotions of the people who live there, to the energetic imprint of guests, and even those who lived there long before us.
I like to begin with sage, followed by palo santo wood. Palo santo is actually my favorite—it brings a sweetness and calm that feels sacred to me. I walk through the entire home, starting at the front door and moving left, circling through each room with the smoke.
It's all about intention. I say things like: "Calling in love and light. Releasing any stuck, heavy, or dense energy from this space." You can invite in whatever support resonates—angels, dragons, golden light, ascended masters, God, Jesus—trust what feels aligned.
Certain rooms, like my son's, tend to hold more activity and energy, so I palo santo them weekly. I always open the windows to let the old energy release and invite in fresh air.

I also keep plenty of plants in the house—they naturally cleanse the air and bring in nature's peace.
And of course, crystals. They hold frequency, beauty, and ancient codes. It's said that in Atlantis, wisdom was embedded into crystals for this very time on Earth! I love Lemurian quartz for this reason.
Singing, dancing, blessing, and simply thanking your home adds to the vibration too. Treat your home like a living being—it will reflect that love right back to you.

Chapter 8: Relationships & Conscious Communication

Let's talk about tuning into your intuition—especially when it comes to relationships. This one is so important these days, and especially within spiritual communities.

Have you ever met someone or spent time with someone and walked away feeling totally drained? Or felt a gut nudge that something just wasn't right? Trust that. That's your body speaking. Your energy doesn't lie.

Boundaries are vital—especially for Starseeds. So many of us are givers. We carry what isn't ours. We try to fix, heal, or hold things that aren't meant to be ours. But part of staying in alignment is learning to discern what is yours... and what is not.

For me, the hardest place to set boundaries has been with my children. I didn't even realize I had no boundaries with them until I began meditating and doing deeper healing work. But slowly, creating gentle boundaries with them has allowed me to carve out space for myself—and that's been life-changing.

Boundaries with friends, family, coworkers—these are all part of what we call spiritual hygiene. It's not always easy, but when you're aligned, everything flows more freely. You'll feel the shift.

When going to crowded places—concerts, events, even the grocery store—I love putting myself and my kids in energy bubbles. For fun, we each choose a color. The kids' colors change often, but I usually go with gold. Diana Cooper teaches that simply imagining golden light around you is enough to keep your energy field strong—so no one can "feed" off your light.

After that, I usually light some palo santo—just because it makes me feel better. It's about what feels good to you. That's what creates protection and clarity in relationships and beyond.

Chapter 9: Nature as Medicine

Now I'm not trying to ruffle any feathers with this one, but in our house—we love the sun. We call it sun therapy. When I'm feeling run-down, when my skin flares up, when I feel disconnected or out of sorts... I go sit in the sun.
Of course, this is easier in sunnier climates—right now as I write this, it's June in California and the weather is just right.
I was raised to fear the sun—always applying sunscreen, covering up, avoiding too much exposure. And I raised my kids that way for a while, too. But now, we practice sun therapy.
We consciously receive the healing light codes from the sun, letting them enter through the top of the head (your crown chakra). It's deeply rejuvenating. It brings clarity, warmth, and recalibration.
That said—always listen to your body. Don't overdo it. Don't burn. I like to use coconut oil on my skin—it's gentle, smells divine, and gives me a bit of natural SPF.

Grounding is another essential practice. Everyone's talking about it for a reason. It's simple: take off your shoes and stand barefoot on the earth. Let your feet touch the soil, grass, sand— anything that connects you back to the living planet.
The earth emits negative ions that help stabilize your nervous system. It's not just spiritual—it's science. You can feel it.

We also love hiking—especially in the trees. Recently, I've been called to sacred rocks. There's something ancient and powerful about placing your hands on stones that have existed for millennia. I like to ask, "Can I merge with you?" And then just feel. Sometimes they sway or pulse back.

You begin to understand: even matter can move. It's a reminder that everything is alive.

And then there's the moon—our beloved cosmic guide.
The full moon is a powerful time for releasing. She helps us let go of what no longer serves. I keep a full moon journal and write down something to release every month.
Right now, I'm on my 18th moon. My goal is 33. I'm clearing everything that's not magical—making space for more magic to flow in.

During the new moon, we call things in. Manifestation flows more easily in this energy. But be mindful—these days, things move fast. When you ask... be ready to receive.

And remember: "The universe only gives you what you believe you are worthy of receiving." — Joe Dispenza

This naturally leads us into our next section...
Daily Rituals.

Chapter 10: Energetic Hygiene & Daily Rituals

So what do I actually do every day that keeps me feeling grounded, aligned, and connected?
Three non-negotiables:
I meditate. I move my body. I eat real food.

I began meditating every morning on January 1st, 2025.
It's the first thing I do when I wake up. I roll out of bed and go straight to my meditation corner. I've made it cozy and sacred— soft pillow, plants, crystals, candles. It's my space to just be.
I do it first thing because if I don't, I'll find ways to put it off. My Kundalini yoga teachers, The Mahanraj's from Great Divine Flow Yoga, talk about healthy suffering. Waking up early to sit in stillness may not always feel easy, but it's a lot easier than the kind of suffering that comes from abandoning yourself.
Sometimes, I'll hit the gym first, but right after, I head into meditation.
Lately, I've been doing Joe Dispenza's work—his meditations focus on connecting with nothingness, or the quantum field where all possibilities exist.
Did I think back in January that I'd be leading monthly women's circles, co-hosting a spiritual retreat, and writing a wellness book?? Absolutely not. But the more I connect with nothing, the more possibilities show up in my life.
At the end of the last chapter, I shared one of my favorite quotes:
"The universe only gives you what you believe you are worthy of receiving."

This changed everything for me.

I spent a full month doing 77-minute meditations focused solely on self-worth—releasing the beliefs I absorbed from family, friends, and society that told me I wasn't enough.

Through yoga, therapy, and now meditation, I've found my worth. It took me 40 years...
Have you found yours yet?

Let me let you in on a little secret:
You are worthy. Of all of it.
And when you *believe* that, the universe responds—with open hands.

Breathwork is another powerful tool. It moves stuck/dense energy and awakens the parts of us that have been asleep. I do intensive breathwork practices a few times a year. It's intense, but so liberating. Most yoga studios or wellness centers offer sessions if you're curious.

Since we are frequency, anything that works with frequency supports the body:
Sound bowls, solfeggio frequency music, tuning forks, movement, voice, and dance. You don't have to be trained. Just *participating* is healing.

I've also become more mindful of my relationship with technology. Taking regular breaks from my phone is a part of my energetic hygiene too. Before I reach for it, I ask: *Is this a true need? Or is it a distraction? A filler?* That moment of awareness shifts everything.

And of course—**food.**

That's the foundation of this entire book.
I only speak from experience: when I eat real food, I feel good.
For years, I didn't even know I felt bad. I drank alcohol, ate processed foods, and lived in a low-vibration state. I was numb.
I was depleted.
Now, I choose real food every day:
My homemade bread, farm eggs, fruits, vegetables, clean meats, chocolate bars, nuts, seeds, and water.
Yes, I still enjoy processed foods now and then—especially when traveling—but my day-to-day is centered on nourishment.

When I stray from this path—eat poorly, skip movement—I feel it *immediately.*
But I don't spiral anymore. I offer myself grace and simply start again the next day.

Meditation, though, is non-negotiable.
That's the anchor of my day, no matter what.

Why would I stop now?
I've only just begun designing the life of my dreams.

Chapter 11: Technology Detox

Screens. Screens. Screens.

As I type this on my computer, talking about screen detox... yes, I feel the irony.

There's a time and place for screens and technology—they're amazing tools when used intentionally. The challenge is being able to only use them when truly needed... not just when we're bored, avoiding emotions, or trying to fill that empty space I mentioned earlier.

We fill that emptiness in so many ways: food, alcohol, TV, iPads, video games.

It's part of our culture.

But as Starseeds—highly sensitive beings—electronics can feel especially draining. They affect our emotional and energetic well-being more than we may realize.

From what I see in today's youth, screens are becoming addictive at younger and younger ages. Violent shows, fast-paced games, overstimulating media... it desensitizes them. It's hard to raise high-frequency kids in a low-frequency world, especially when technology is constantly pulling at their attention.

Right now, we're in a digital detox in our home.

That means no video games, no iPad shows or movies.

Just one family movie on the weekend—if we feel called.

We're doing this for about a month, and I can already see the shifts—especially in my son's emotional well-being.

I'm not a neuroscientist, and I don't know all the developmental science behind it... but I do know addiction.

I know what it's like to crave something that takes you out of the present moment. And let's be honest—screens feel good. They help us zone out. They help us escape. That's okay sometimes, if used with awareness.

In hard seasons, we've leaned on screens for survival. And I don't carry guilt for that. But when life feels more stable—when my cup is full—I do my best to reset our rhythm. And a digital detox is part of that.

I also try to be mindful of EMFs—those invisible waves that radiate from electronics. I don't let my kids hold iPads or laptops directly on their laps. I'm not living in fear, but I *am* aware. If your device is getting hot, that heat is transferring to the body. And our children's systems are still developing. These things matter—especially as technology gets more powerful with every new release.

I try to keep a healthy ratio. If I've spent a few hours on my laptop writing or creating, I balance it with time outside, time in nature, or time just being present without screens.

In our Sacred Sister Ceremonies, we often talk about the transition from the Piscean Age to the Aquarian Age. We've been in the Piscean Age for over 2,000 years, and now we're emerging into a new frequency. One of the biggest themes of the Aquarian Age?

Technology.

Use it wisely. Use it as a tool to enhance your life. But *do not* let it consume your life force. If you feel yourself—or your little Starseeds—getting pulled too far into the screen world… take a *Sacred Pause.* Reflect. Journal. Go outside. Do something that reconnects you to your body and your spirit. And when you return to your screens, do it with intention.

Chapter 12: Conscious Threads

Clothing, Color, and Frequency

Since everything holds a frequency—what we eat, what we listen to, what we watch, what we wash our clothes with—it only makes sense that what we wear matters too.

This is a subject I'm both passionate about and tender with. Because I get it—not everyone can afford high-vibrational fabrics. Polyester is cheap and everywhere. It's widely used for a reason.

But here's what we need to know: Polyester is synthetic. It's made from petroleum-based chemicals. So are nylon, acrylic, and spandex. These are not natural fibers. They carry the frequency of zero.

Natural fabrics, on the other hand—cotton, organic cotton, linen, hemp, and wool—hold much higher vibrations.

- Linen and wool are said to vibrate around 5,000 MHz.
- Cotton holds a frequency around 100 MHz.
- Organic cotton is slightly higher.
- Polyester? Zero.

Everything we do either adds to or subtracts from our frequency.

When I'm doing inner work, meditating, or just needing a pick-me-up, I wear linen. I even invested in linen sheets—and wow, the dreams we had in those first few weeks were next-level!

This can be especially important for sensitive Starseed children and adults.

My whole family (even our dog!) has sensitive skin. Cotton is always the most comfortable for us. When I find organic cotton, even better.

Linen and wool hold the highest frequency in fabric—around 5,000 MHz—while polyester holds a vibration of zero. It's no wonder linen has long been considered sacred.
In fact, linen is mentioned in the Bible over 100 times, used for holy garments, sacred rituals, and healing cloths.
If it's good enough for Jesus, it's certainly good enough for me.

And no—you don't need to throw out every petroleum-based piece of clothing you own. That would be extreme. We want balance, not panic. What I do is stay mindful. When I shop, I usually choose the cotton or linen-blend option instead of polyester.
I also love buying secondhand. A lot of the chemicals have been washed out, and it's a more sustainable way to shop. Sure, some residues like PFAS (forever chemicals) may still remain—but in lesser amounts. For a while, I even ran a small clothing line made entirely of natural fabrics. It was beautiful. It felt good. And it vibrated high.

And then there's color.
Our bodies have energy centers—chakras—and each one is associated with a color. When we want to connect with or support a certain part of ourselves, we can wear that color to enhance the frequency.
Here are a few examples:

ॐ Violet/White - connection to self and the divine.
ॐ Indigo - intuition and trust.
ह Aqua Blue – for communication and truth.
ऊ Green – for love and the heart.
ऱ Yellow- confidence and personal power.
द Orange – for creativity and sexuality.
व Red – for grounding and stability.

And yes, this goes for food too!
The colors of the food we eat influence our energy centers—
especially when we eat with intention.
Want to feel more rooted? Roast some red beets (recipe in part
3). Want to boost your sensual energy? Add more orange foods
like sweet potatoes or mangoes to your plate.

Lastly, let's talk about totems.

I wear sacred symbols on my body every day—my cross
necklace, Metatron's cube, the tree of life, dragon rings, and
crystal bracelets. They're not just beautiful—they're intentional.
These totems help me feel anchored, protected, and spiritually
aligned.

Symbolism carries power.
Wear what speaks to your soul.

Chapter 13: Financial Frequency

Let's talk about abundance mindset. Many of us were raised with a scarcity mindset — the belief that there's never enough: food, money, love, time, or security. This mindset served a real purpose for past generations — for those who survived the Great Depression, and for humanity as a whole during the last 2,000 years of the Piscean Age. But as we shift into the Aquarian Age, our beliefs, thoughts, and values around abundance and money must shift too.

The universe will always provide what I need. If I need or desire more, I will ask. I truly believe that before we came here, in heaven or in another dimension, we helped write our soul's journey — our soul contract. Now that I'm in my happiness era, I know I wrote myself a beautiful life, one filled with love, protection, and abundance. So, do we simply walk our path and trust that all of our soul's agreements will fall into place? You can do that. Or you can put some action behind it.

A beautiful tool I use is the 369 journal practice. My dear friend Tiffany introduced this to me. It's based on the wisdom of Nikola Tesla and the Law of Attraction. You can order a 369 journal on Amazon and get started anytime — though I love to begin on a new moon. If you want to layer in even more magic, align your intention with the energy of the new moon sign:

New Moon in Virgo — start new habits or daily routines
New Moon in Leo — begin something visible, & rewarding
New Moon in Libra — call in balance, harmony, & beauty

As I write this, I'm looking forward to starting my next 369 journal on the New Moon in Cancer in a few days.
Whether you choose to journal or not, I encourage you to be mindful of how you think and speak about money.
Money is just energy. It comes and goes. The more we focus on lack, the more lack we experience.

Energy flows where attention goes. So focus on your dreams. The ones you had as a child before anyone told you they weren't possible. And remember, as Roald Dahl said: "Those who don't believe in magic will never find it."

Miracles are happening all around us — stay open, stay believing.

Chapter 14: Conscious Parenting & LIfestyle Choices

I'm not a parenting expert — I only speak from experience, intuition, and the guidance of trusted mentors. There are a few things we do daily to help keep our spiritual and energy hygiene clear.

On the way to school, we sing mantras. We listen to mantra music — usually (but not always) in Sanskrit, an ancient sacred language. When we sing these mantras, I feel our frequency lift immediately. It's a beautiful way to activate our throat chakras and speak words that carry healing vibrations. I love hearing my kids sing in the car; I believe it helps them build confidence to speak up in more difficult moments.

Of course, leaving the house isn't always as smooth as I'd like — sometimes there's rushing, raised voices, tears, or a last-minute bathroom trip just as we're loading up the car. The drive to school becomes a chance to recalibrate, to soothe and reset their nervous systems if the morning didn't unfold as I intended. Chanting and mantra help bring us back to equilibrium so they can step into their day peacefully.

Our own voices are the most comforting, healing sound to our bodies — so the more singing, the better!

For me, singing mantras is an instant connection to Source, to my soul. I often remind women in my sister circles: even if your human self doesn't know the words, your soul has sung this song before. I'll never forget one of my first spiritual aha moments while singing the mantra Sat Kartar — full body tingles, a sense of home, deep love in my heart, and a connection to myself I'd never felt before.

Beyond all of that, mantras clear stuck energy, open the heart, bring brain waves into coherence, fill us with life force, and simply feel so good.

At night, we do prayers, invocations, and gratitude.
We start with invocations — I am statements focused on what we need most in that moment: I am strong. I am smart. I am worthy. I love myself. Then we move into gratitude. As Dr. Joe Dispenza says, "Gratitude is the ultimate state of receivership." We give thanks for our blessings, and it always feels like more come our way.

We also clear energy at bedtime. Sometimes we use tuning forks, because they're fun and easy for the kids to use. Other times, we do a simple raking of the energy field — starting at the head and sweeping down the aura until it feels complete. A fun game we play is having them close their eyes and tell me when they can "feel" my hands in their field — often 6 to 12 inches away from their body!

I believe how we start and end our days really matters, so I try to be intentional. I don't always have the energy to guide everything, so I'm teaching my kids how to do these things themselves. A peaceful transition into the sleep realm is always my intention. After all, we spend half of our lives "asleep" — or on the other side — and half "awake." My hope is that these simple practices help my children (and myself) move between these worlds with ease, feeling safe, grounded, and connected to who they truly are.
I believe these little rituals help their energy flow freely into creativity and curiosity.

Bedtime Blessings

"May we enter the dream realm with peace in our hearts, protected, guided, and wrapped in the light of love. May our souls remember who we are, and may we awaken renewed, connected, and ready to walk this world with grace".

"I am grateful for the blessings of today and look forward to the opportunities of tomorrow".

"I invoke Archangel Michael's deep blue pyramid of protection around my home while I sleep".

Chapter 15: How We Eat

Before we dive into the recipes, I want to share a little bit about how we eat in our home. Our meals aren't fancy—they're intentional, clean, and made with love. The recipes you'll find here are versatile. You can swap in what works for you—meat or veggie, grains or greens. This is about nourishment, not perfection.

Sundays are often our prep days. We'll make a big lentil stew or stir fry to carry us through the week. It's such a gift to have something already made on those extra full days. Sometimes we repurpose leftovers by frying an egg on top or tossing them into a bowl with fresh quinoa or rice and a sautéed veggie. Other nights, we grill some clean burgers and throw together a simple side.

The focus is always the same: simple, clean, high-frequency ingredients. Eating this way helps our bodies stay clear and grounded while still anchoring in the higher energies that are streaming onto the planet right now.

And of course—flavor matters. We love using coconut aminos, cashew crema, and homemade vinaigrettes to brighten up any dish. Store-bought salad dressings, even the pricey ones, often sneak in low-vibe seed oils. A homemade dressing is such an easy upgrade.

This section is here to remind you that eating well doesn't have to be complicated. Let your food feel good. Let it support your light.

A Note on Ingredients

We do our best to eat organic, local, and high-vibrational foods whenever possible.

Chapter 16: Intuition, Energy, & Trust

In this book, I've spoken often about following your intuition. But what does that really mean? How do we know what's intuition—and what's just noise?

To be honest, it's taken me many years to trust myself—in the kitchen, and in life.

When it comes to cooking, I've found it's best to feel your way through it. Not everyone moves like my husband, who can somehow cook five things at once and make it look effortless. For most of us, it's best to start simple.

I like to make a meal a few times and tweak it each time to fit what feels good in my body. I find a recipe that uses ingredients aligned with my vibration, and then I build from there. Once I've got a couple of meals down and tasting great, I'll move on to something new.

I never force myself to cook something I don't want to make. If my energy is low, I go easy. We love to prep extra veggies and meats on Sundays so we can just sauté them together later in the week for quick, nourishing meals.

When my energy is high—usually during the second and third weeks of my cycle—I cook a lot! That's when I'll experiment or try something new. My daughter and I often play around in the kitchen, creating healthy treats like our chocolate bread, gluten-free cookies, or homemade granola.

Listening to your energy is one of the best cooking tips I can give. Don't attempt a complex recipe when you're tired, PMS-ing, or running on no sleep. Honor your body. Even in the kitchen.

As for intuition in life... it comes back to the same thing: trust yourself. That's the lesson I keep being handed over and over—trust.

Trust your feelings.
Trust your limits.
Trust your children.

Children are incredibly wise these days. They often *know*. If your intuitive child turns down a food, give them the benefit of the doubt. Offer something else that's nourishing.
Honestly, it was my children who opened me to my own intuition. Birthing them awakened my belief in God, in myself, and in the quiet knowing that the Universe always supports us. Our needs will always be met.
After surviving my twenties—truly surviving—I now know without a doubt:
I am divinely guided. I am protected. And so are you.
This faith allows me to live more fully. To trust that everything is divinely timed. To see everyday as sacred. To cook, to parent, to pray, to simply *be*—from a place of trust.

So as you walk your own path of remembrance, May you tune in to your own inner wisdom. May you trust your energy, follow your intuition, and live in the truth that you are always held.

Take care of your vessel. It's what allows us to be human. I truly believe we are spiritual beings having a human experience—and the healthier our human vessel is, the easier and more joyful our journey can be.

Part Three

Nourishment For the Starseed Body

Foundations: Broths, Beans, Grains

J & Q's Golden Bone Broth

RICH, GROUNDING, AND FULL OF LIFE FORCE—THIS BROTH IS A STAPLE IN ANY HIGH-FREQUENCY KITCHEN.

INGREDIENTS

1-2 Chicken backs

1-2 beef knuckles

Garlic head

1 small ginger chunk

1 medium turmeric chunk

3-4 Carrots

1 large Onion

1 small bulb Fennel (omit if you prefer a richer flavor)

Fresh thyme, oregano, rosemary

1 tbsp salt

Pinch of Peppercorn

DIRECTIONS

- Chop your vegetables into large chunks. No need to peel—just rinse well.
- Place all ingredients into the Instant Pot insert.
- Fill with water until it reaches the "Max Fill" line inside the pot.
- Select "Pressure Cook" on your Instant Pot.
- Set the timer for 2 hours and 15 minutes (02:15).
- When the cooking time is complete, let the pressure release naturally. This may take 20–30 minutes.
- Strain the broth into a large bowl using a fine mesh strainer. Discard the solids or compost them.
- Let the broth cool, then pour into glass jars or containers.
- Store in the fridge for up to 1 week, or freeze for longer storage (up to several months).

Garbanzo Beans

Directions

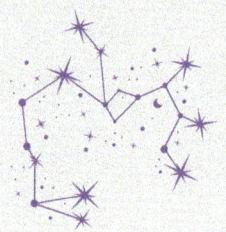

- ◇ How to Cook Dried Garbanzo Beans
- Ingredients:
- 1 ½ cups dried garbanzo beans
- Water for soaking and cooking
- ½ tsp sea salt (optional)
- Instructions:
- Soak Overnight:
- Place the dried garbanzo beans in a large bowl and cover them with plenty of water. Soak for at least 8 hours or overnight. They will expand, so make sure there's room and extra water.
- Drain + Rinse:
- After soaking, drain the beans and rinse them well under cool water.
- Cook:
- Add beans to a large pot and cover with fresh water (about 2 inches above the beans). Bring to a boil, then reduce heat to low and simmer.
- Simmer Gently:
- Let the beans cook uncovered for 45–60 minutes, or until they are soft but not falling apart. Skim off any foam if needed.
- Season:
- For Nourishing bowls, add sea salt, pepper, paprika, chipotle pepper, cumin or any other seasonings you prefer in the last 10 minutes of cooking. (Adding it earlier can make beans tougher.)
- Drain + Use:
- Once cooked, drain the beans. They're now ready to be added to bowls, salads, or blended into dips

Notes

You can also use a tetrapak or can of garbanzo beans (I avoid cans because of the aluminum) that are already cooked. Just reheat with about ¼ cup water add add seasoning. Good in fridge for about a week..

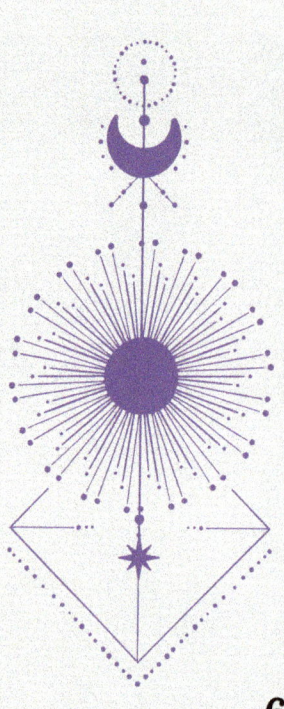

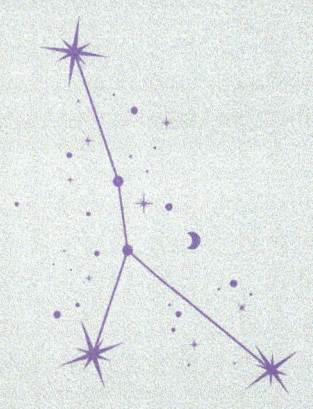

Ghee Rice

INGREDIENTS

1 cup organic white rice (basmati, jasmine)

1.5 cups of water (follow amount on rice bag)

2 tbsp ghee

½ tsp salt

DIRECTIONS

1. Rinse the rice in cool water until the water runs clear. This removes extra starch and helps the rice cook fluffy.
2. In a medium pot, bring the water to a boil.
3. Once boiling, add the ghee and salt.
4. Stir in the rice. Reduce heat to low, cover with a lid, and let simmer for 15–18 minutes (or follow the instructions on your rice package).
5. Turn off the heat and let the rice sit (still covered) for 5 minutes.
6. Fluff with a fork and enjoy!

NOTES

Add chopped cilantro to make cilantro rice
Add zest of a lemon to make lemon rice

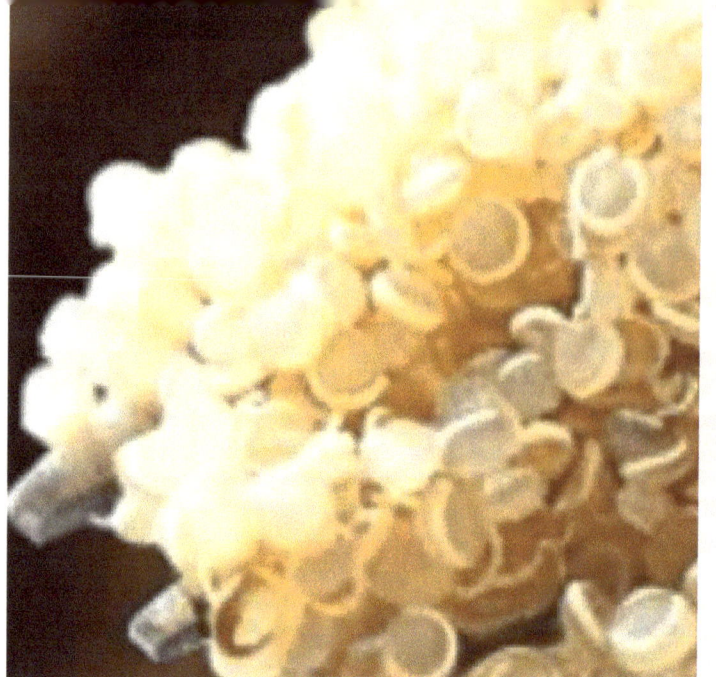

Bone Broth Quinoa

1 cup quinoa

2 cups bone broth

DIRECTIONS

1. Rinse the quinoa:
2. Place quinoa in a fine mesh strainer and rinse under cool water for 30 seconds to remove bitterness.

Cook:

1. In a saucepan, combine rinsed quinoa and bone broth.
2. Simmer:
3. Bring to a gentle boil, then reduce heat to low. Cover and let simmer for 15 minutes.
4. Rest:
5. Remove from heat and let sit (still covered) for 5 minutes.
6. Fluff + Serve:
7. Use a fork to fluff the quinoa. Serve warm, or let cool for bowls and salads.

Optional:

1. Add a drizzle of olive oil, a squeeze of lemon, or chopped herbs for extra vibrance.
2. If prapering quinoa with water, just add a pinch of salt to the boiling water.

*Though we often treat it like a grain, quinoa is actually a seed from the chenopod plant, making it a pseudograin. It's naturally gluten-free, high in protein, and contains all nine essential amino acids—making it a rare plant-based complete protein.

64

A Note on Bread Making

Bread making takes practice, patience, and a willingness to tune into your baking intuition. Each loaf is a chance to learn—especially with the Basically White Loaf, which can vary in proofing time depending on the season.
In warmer summer months, your starter may be more active, shortening the rise time. During winter, things tend to slow down. This means proofing can range anywhere from 4 to 10 hours on the counter. You can also refrigerate your dough and bake it later—just remember, it still needs to rise before going into the oven.
To speed things up, place your loaf in the oven on the "proof" setting and cover it with plastic wrap to keep it from drying out. You'll know your bread is ready to bake when the dough rises to the edge of the baking pan.

For the Basically Awesome Loaf, even after refrigeration, it usually only needs about 2.5 to 4 hours of proof time.
You'll know it's ready when the dough feels soft and slightly springy to the touch. If it feels too soft or puffy, it may be overproofed—but don't worry, this is where your baking intuition starts to develop. Remember, it's bread… so it's good either way. Trust the process and enjoy what it teaches you.

Before baking, score your bread.
You can make a simple slice down the center or get creative with beautiful designs—both are perfect.

In the following recipes, I'll walk you through the process of breadmaking, but I won't stress every single detail. That's intentional.

When I first started baking, I obsessed over every step and missed the chance to truly trust myself.

Baking is deeply intuitive. You learn by doing. Sometimes things won't turn out—and that's okay. "Failure" is just the recipe teaching you something new.

And if you ever feel stuck or unsure, please reach out on Instagram @knowbysoul or email knowyoursoul.yogi@gmail.com —I'm always happy to support you on your journey.

I personally use 1 lb loaf pans from USA Pan American, and they work beautifully for this recipe.

Gluten-Free Sourdough Starter

How to Make a Sourdough Starter
From scratch—or order some of mine!
You only need two ingredients:
gluten free flour + water
That's it. I use high quality organic brown ric
Feel free to try a different type of gluten free

Step 1: Mix
In a clean glass jar, stir together:
- ½ cup flour
- ½ cup water (room temp)

Mix until smooth. It should be a little thicker than pancake batter.
👉 If it feels too thick, add a splash of water.
👉 Too runny? Sprinkle in more flour.
Loosely cover with a lid or towel. Don't seal it tight—your starter needs air!
Leave it on the counter for 24 hours.

Step 2: Feed
The next day, open the jar. You might not see much yet—don't worry!
- Scoop out half of the mixture and toss it (or compost it).
- Add in ½ cup flour + ½ cup water
- Mix it up again. Cover loosely.
- Leave on the counter another 24 hours.

Step 3: Repeat
Do the same thing every day:
➤ Toss half,
➤ Feed with flour + water,
➤ Mix and let it sit.

After a few days, you'll see bubbles forming—this means your starter is waking up and coming alive!

Tips as It Grows
- Once you see bubbles, you can use less flour and water to avoid wasting ingredients.
- After about a week, your starter will get stronger and more bubbly.
- You can now feed every other day if you like.

When It's Ready to Bake
When it bubbles within 3-5 hours after feeding, it's ready to use!
In warm weather, it rises faster.
In cooler months, it might take longer.
Here in California in June, I feed it in the morning—and it's usually ready to bake by mid-afternoon! A

Mature
Once your starter is about 2 weeks old and bubbly, store it in the fridge between bakes.
Just take it out, feed it, and let it warm up again when you're ready to bake.

Final Thoughts
Making sourdough is like tending to a new little pet.
Be patient. Be curious.
Have fun and trust your intuition.
Each starter has its own personality—and yours will grow with love.

Basically Awesome Gluten-Free Sourdough Loaf

Instructions:

- Mix the dry ingredients: In a large bowl, whisk together the flours and salt.
- Mix the wet ingredients: In a separate bowl, combine water, honey (or syrup), oil, and yeast. Stir until the yeast dissolves.
- Combine wet and dry: Pour the wet mixture into the dry ingredients. Stir well until everything is evenly combined. The dough will be slightly sticky.
- Gently knead the dough on a clean surface for about 1 minute. Shape it into a loaf.
- Grease a loaf pan with avocado oil spray.
- Place the dough into the pan, then loosely seal the whole pan inside a large ziplock bag or cover with a damp cloth.

- Choose your rise method:
- For baking later: Place the covered dough in the fridge overnight.
- For same-day baking: Let it rise on the counter for about 3 hours (a little longer in colder months).
- Bake the loaf:
  - Preheat oven to 425°F.
  - Bake for 35 minutes.
  - Lower the oven to 400°F and bake for another 35 minutes.
  - Carefully remove the loaf from the pan and place directly on the oven rack.
  - Bake for a final 10–12 minutes, until the loaf is golden and firm to the touch.
- Cool completely: Let the bread cool for at least a few hours before slicing—it finishes setting as it rests.

Ingredients:

- 70g sorghum flour
- 70g buckwheat flour
- 70g tapioca starch
- 60g brown rice flour
- 30g pumpkin seed flour
- 10g salt
- 20g flaxseed meal
- 20g psyllium husk
- 20g honey or maple syrup
- 150g starter
- 350g water

Basically White Gluten-Free Sourdough

Directions

- Mix dry ingredients
- Add all your dry ingredients to the bowl of a stand mixer.
- Mix wet ingredients
- In a separate bowl, stir together all the wet ingredients.
- Combine
- Pour the wet ingredients into the dry. Mix with the stand mixer for about 7 minutes, until the dough is smooth and well combined.
- Prepare the bread pan
- Lightly grease or spray your bread pan.
- Add dough to pan
- Scoop the dough into the pan. Use a spatula to spread it evenly and smooth the top.
- Proof the dough
- Let the dough rise (proof) either: In the fridge overnight or on the counter for 4–10 hours, until it rises near the top of the pan.
- Score the bread
- Just before baking, use a sharp knife to make a shallow cut (score) along the top of the dough. This helps control how it expands in the oven.
- Bake: Bake at 350°F (175°C) for 70 minutes.
- Finish baking
- Carefully remove the bread from the pan. Place it directly on the oven rack and bake for another 11 minutes, or until the crust is golden brown.
- Cool completely
- Let the bread cool for at least 8 hours before slicing. This helps set the crumb and makes slicing easier.

Ingredients

- 248g Namaste gluten-free flour blend
- 124g Potato Starch (potato alternative tapioca starch)
- 10g salt
- 8g xanthum gum
- 20g flaxseed meal
- 60g olive oil
- 15g maple syrup
- 150g sourdough starter
- 350g water

72

Basically Chocolate Bread (adapted from Basically White Bread)

Ingredients

Changes to ingredients:

- Minus 50g potato starch and add 50g unsweetened cocoa powder
- Add 20-40g more maple syrup for sweeter bread
- Add 20g more olive oil
- Consider adding 1 teaspoon vanilla extract for extra depth
- fold in dark chocolate chips (about 1/2 cup) if you want a double chocolate vibe
- salt (optional)

Directions

1. Sift or whisk the cocoa powder with your dry ingredients to evenly distribute it.
2. Add your sweetener and vanilla to the wet ingredients.
3. Sprinkle salt on warm loaf

Large loaf:
Proof until risen (on the counter or using your oven's proof setting). Bake at 350°F for 70 minutes.
Muffins:
Proof in the oven on proof setting for a few hours. Bake at 350°F for about 60 minutes.
Mini loaves:
Proof as above. Bake at 350°F for 45-60 minutes, or until golden and cooked through.

Gluten-Free Sourdough Waffles

These are a beautiful breakfast or dinner idea! Waffles are delicious fresh or frozen. We keep several in the freezer for quik snacks or meals.

Ingredients

- 200g sourdough discard
- 200g coconut milk
- 50g honey
- 1 egg
- 40g melted coconut oil
- 20g flaxseed meal
- ¼ tsp salt
- 20g sorghum flour
- 70-90g buckwheat flour

Instructions:

- Plug in Belgium waffle maker
- Mix egg, milk, starter, honey, flaxseed and melted coconut oil
- Mix the flours and salt
- Whisk all ingredients together
- Use ¾ cup scoop for batter
- Cook until golden brown
- Makes about 6-7 waffles
- Enjoy!
- Store leftovers in fridge or freezer

Notes:

Adjust consistency to preference. Add more milk for thinner, crispier waffles. Add more discard for thicker waffles.

Sunrise Stackers

Gluten-Free. Vegan. Totally Celestial.

These pancakes are vegan,
but if you're not plant-based, you can
easily swap the
flaxseed meal for 1 egg.

Kitchen Alchemy Note:
If you use sunbutter (sunflower seed butter), don't be
surprised if your pancakes turn a subtle green after a while.
This is a natural reaction between the chlorophyll in
sunflower seeds and the baking soda—completely safe and still
delicious.
Just a little kitchen magic!

Ingredients

2 cups buckwheat flour

1 tsp baking soda

1 tsp salt

½ tsp cinnamon

2 cups nut milk

2 tbsp flaxseed meal

1 tsp vanilla

2 tbsp honey

3 tbsp coconut oil, melted

Method

1. Preheat cast iton skillet on low/medium
2. In a mixing bowl, whisk together the nut
   flaxseed meal, vanilla, honey, and melted
   coconut oil until the honey dissolves
   completely.
3. Let the wet mixture sit for 5 minutes to a
   the flax to bind and slightly thicken.
4. In a separate bowl, combine the buckwhe
   flour, baking soda, salt, and cinnamon.
5. Pour the wet ingredients into the dry and
   until just combined.
6. Add 2 tbsp melted coconut oil to batter a
   mix immediately while oil is warm and m
7. Add small amount of coconut oil to heate
   skillet.
8. Scoop batter (about 1/3 cup per pancake)
   the skillet. Cook for about 3 minutes until
   bubbles form, then flip and cook for anot
   4 minutes.
9. Serve warm with fresh fruit, chopped nuts
   drizzle of maple syrup, or your favorite co
   toppings.

Sacred Stuffing

INGREDIENTS

1 loaf gluten-free
sourdough loaf
(dried and cubed)
1 medium onion,
chopped
4 stalks celery,
chopped
4 cloves garlic,
minced
fresh mixed herbs,
chopped (sage,
thyme, light
rosemary)
2 tsp salt
pepper to taste
1 stick Miyokos dairy
free butter or
regular butter
 1-2 cups bone broth
2 cups chopped
pecans
1 cup dried cherries,
unsweetened

DIRECTIONS

1. Prep Bread: Cube the sourdough loaf and let it dry out overnight, or toast it in the oven at 300°F for 15–20 minutes until lightly crisp but not browned.
2. In a large mixing bowl, combine bread, onion, celery, garlic, herbs, salt & pepper.
3. Melt butter in pan and add to mixture. Mix well
4. Slowly pour in 1 cup of bone broth and gently toss everything together. If the mixture seems too dry, add more broth a little at a time until it's moist but not soggy.
5. Add cherry and pecans. Mix
6. Cover in refrigerator overnight (a few hours is fine)
7. Bake: Transfer stuffing to a baking dish. Bake at 350 for 25 mins.
8. Remove and mix. Cook for additional 25 minutes or until the top is golden and crisp.
9. Serve Warm: Best served with gravy. Enjoy!

Conscious Meats

INGREDIENTS

- 8 eggs
- ½ cup milk
- salt & pepper to taste
- 1 tbsp ghee or avocado oil
- 1 bag arugula
- seasonal veggies (zucchini, onion, mushrooms, my favorite is kale and zucchini)
- keep it veggie or add cooked meat of choice (ground beef, bison, chorizo)

INSTRUCTIONS

1. Preheat oven to 350°F.
2. Cook the meat:
3. In a skillet (or separate pan if you prefer less fat in your frittata), cook the meat until fully done. Set aside.
4. Sauté veggies: In your cast iron skillet, heat avocado oil over medium heat.
5. Add veggies and sauté 5–7 minutes until softened.
6. Whisk eggs: In a bowl, whisk eggs, coconut milk, salt, and pepper until well combined.
7. Assemble: Add the cooked meat to the veggies in the cast iron skillet.
8. Pour the egg mixture evenly over everything.
9. Let it cook on the stovetop for about 2–3 minutes — just until the edges start to set.
10. Finish in oven: Transfer the skillet to the oven. Bake 10–15 minutes, or until the eggs are set in the center and slightly golden on top.
11. Serve: Cool slightly, slice, and enjoy! Top with arugula, fresh herbs, avocado, or a squeeze of lemon..

Cosmic Garden Frittata

This frittata is a crowd favorite in our home.
We eat it for breakfast, lunch, or dinner —any time we want something nourishing, grounding, and delicious.
It's easy to make your own. Enjoy it with any variety of vegetables and meat that calls to you. Top it with cashew crema for a creamy, high-vibe finish.
Simple. Satisfying. Made with love.

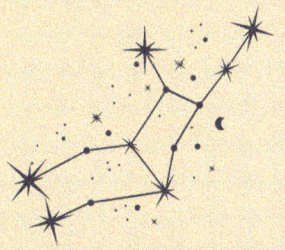

Ingredients

Wild salmon fillets

1 cedar plank soaked in
water for at least one
hour

Salt and pepper

3 tbsp Coconut aminos

2 tbsp Maple syrup

Juice from 1 Lime

Lime or lemon slices

*Pairs well with ghee rice
and roasted cauliflower*

Plank Roasted Salmon with Maple Glaze

Method

1. Preheat your smoker or BBQ to 350°F.
2. Generously season the salmon filet with salt and pepper.
3. In a small bowl, mix together the coconut aminos, maple syrup, and lime juice.
4. Brush the mixture all over the salmon filet.
5. Place sliced citrus on top of the salmon.
6. Set the salmon on a cedar plank in smoker.
7. Roast for 15–20 minutes, or until the salmon flakes easily with a fork.
8. For accuracy, check that the internal temperature reaches about 125°F.
9. Let rest for a few mins. Enjoy!

The Rebel Loaf

INGREDIENTS

1 lb bison or grass fed
Beef

1 egg

1/2 bell pepper, chopped

1/2 onion, chopped

2 garlic cloves ,minced

1/3 cup gluten-free bread
crumbs

3 tbsp bbq sauce

1tsp salt & pepper

Extra bbq sauce or
ketchup for glazing

DIRECTIONS

1. In a large bowl, combine the ground meat, egg, bell pepper, onion, garlic, breadcrumbs, BBQ sauce, salt, and pepper.
2. Mix everything well using clean hands or a spoon.
3. Once combined, shape the mixture into a football-style loaf.
4. Preheat your smoker or BBQ to 350°F.
5. Place the meatloaf directly onto the smoker grate.
6. Cook for 25 minutes.
7. Brush the top of the meatloaf with extra BBQ sauce or ketchup.
8. Continue cooking for another 25 minutes, or until the internal temperature reaches 145–155°F.
9. Let it rest for about 5–10 minutes before slicing.
10. Enjoy! Perfect with roasted veggies or a crisp salad

85

THE ANCESTRAL PATTY

Ingredients

- 1 lb ground bison
- Salt (to taste)
- Garlic powder (to taste)
- Black pepper (to taste)
- Smoked paprika (to taste)
- A few dashes of coconut aminos

Directions

1. Thaw the bison if it's frozen. Let it come to room temperature for even cooking.
2. Shape the meat into patties — we like them large and thin for a quick sear and juicy center.
3. Season one side of each patty with salt, garlic powder, and black pepper.
4. Flip the patties and season the other side with salt, smoked paprika, and a light drizzle of coconut aminos.
5. Grill or pan-fry the burgers over medium-high heat for about 4 minutes per side. Bison cooks quickly, so don't overdo it!
6. Let rest for 2–3 minutes before serving.

Notes: pairs well with quinoa and grilled veggies

Teriyaki Bison

Ingredients

- 1 lb ground bison
- 1 onion, chopped
- 6 cloves garlic, minced
- 1 thumb-sized chunk fresh ginger, peeled and minced
- 3 tbsp soy-free teriyaki sauce (we love Big Tree Farms brand)
- Salt and pepper to taste

Directions

- Chop the onion, garlic, and ginger. Set aside.
- Heat a pan over medium heat. Add a little oil if needed.
- Sauté the onion, garlic, and ginger for 3–4 minutes, until soft and fragrant. Season with a pinch of salt and pepper.
- Add the ground bison to the pan. Break it apart with a spatula and cook for about 3 minutes.

- Pour in the teriyaki sauce, stir well, and cook for another 5–8 minutes, or until the bison is fully cooked through (no pink left).
- Taste and adjust seasoning if needed. Serve warm and enjoy!

Notes: Pairs well with roasted cauliflower and quinoa

Vibrant Veggies

INGREDIENTS

- Several heads of radicchio (quartered or halved, depending on size)
- Your favorite blue cheese or dairy-free cheese alternative
- Olive oil or another high-quality oil (for brushing)
- Salt and pepper, to taste
- Honey (for drizzling)

INSTRUCTIONS

1. Prepare the grill — Preheat your grill to medium-high heat.
2. Prep the radicchio — Brush the cut sides of the radicchio with oil. Sprinkle with salt and pepper.
3. Grill — Place radicchio cut-side down on the grill. Cook for 3–5 minutes per side, or until lightly charred and softened.
4. Top + serve — Remove from the grill. While warm, sprinkle generously with blue cheese and drizzle with honey.
5. Enjoy — Serve as is, or pile onto slices of well-toasted gluten-free sourdough bread.

Sweet & Funky Grilled Radicchio

These make a funky and delicious snack, appetizer, or addition to any meal. Enjoy the bold, vibrant flavors together!

Ingredients:

1-2 heads cauliflower

2 tbsp coconut oil or
ghee

salt to taste

Roasted Cauliflower

Directions:

1. Remove the outer leaves from the cauliflower and trim the stem, but keep the core intact. The core helps hold the steaks together.
2. Place the cauliflower core-side down on a cutting board.
3. Using a large, sharp knife, slice the cauliflower straight down into slabs about ½ to ¾ inch thick. Start from the center and work outward.
4. You'll likely get 2-3 intact "steaks" from the center. The sides will break into florets—that's totally normal! Roast them alongside your steaks.
5. Place cauliflower steaks on a large baking sheet covered with parchment. Drizzle with oil. Sprinkle with salt and any additional seasonings (turmeric powder is really good, just be mindful it stains). Toss well to coat evenly.
6. Roast: Spread the florets out in a single layer (avoid crowding the pan so they crisp up).
7. Roast for 25–30 minutes, flipping halfway through, until golden and slightly crisp on the edges.
8. Serve & Enjoy!

Roasted Broccolini with Garlic

Ingredients

- 1-2 bunches of broccolini, washed and trimmed
- 3 cloves garlic
- garlic press
- 2 tbsp ghee or coconut oil
- salt & pepper to taste

Directions

1. Heat oven to 325
2. Line cookie sheet with parchment. Place broccolini on sheet
3. Smash garlic cloves with garlic press and mix with coconut oil or ghee
4. Spread mixture onto broccoli
5. Mix up well
6. Cook for 10 mins
7. Rotate and mix- cook additional 10 mins or until ends are crisp and lightly golden

Luminous Greens-
Teriyaki Kale

Ingredients

1 bunch kale
1 tbsp coconut oil,
ghee, or sesame oil
2 tbsp soy free
teriyaki sauce
1 clove garlic minced
(optional)
salt & pepper to taste

This is a salty, satisfying side that pairs beautifully with almost any dish. The kale soaks up the teriyaki for the perfect mix of savory, nourishing, and vibrant. Quick to make, easy to love.

Method

1. Heat the oil in a large skillet over medium heat.
2. Sauté aromatics (if using): Add garlic cook for about 30 seconds until fragrant.
3. Add kale: Toss in the chopped kale. Sauté for about 3–5 minutes, stirring occasionally, until it's bright green and just tender.
4. Add teriyaki: Drizzle in teriyaki sauce. Stir to coat evenly. Let it cook for another minute so the sauce soaks in.
5. Serve & Enjoy!

Roasted Beet salad

INGREDIENTS

1 bunch of beets
1 head fresh lettuce
½ cup chopped pecans
1 shaved carrot
½ cup crumbled goat cheese
¼ cup hemp seeds
1–2 cups chopped roasted beets (about 2–3 medium beets)
¼ cup pumpkin seeds
Vinegriette

DIRECTIONS

1. Preheat your oven to 375°F (190°C).
2. Prepare the beets: Chop off the beet greens and the bottom of the beets. Place them in a baking dish with about 1 inch of water.
3. Cover and bake for 45 minutes, or until the beets are tender when pierced with a fork.
4. Cool the beets in the fridge. Once cooled, wear gloves (to avoid staining your hands) and peel off the beet skin.Prepare the salad: While the beets cool, chop the lettuce and place it in a large salad bowl.
5. Add the toppings: Toss in the pecans, carrots, goat cheese, hemp seeds, and pumpkin seeds.
6. Chop the beets into bite-sized pieces and add them to the salad.
7. Add vinegriettte
8. Serve and enjoy!

Vegan Delights

Zucchini & Black Bean Tacos

INGREDIENTS

1 tbsp avocado oil

1 avocado

1 tetrapak black beans

1 bunch cilantro

2 tbsp crema

1 zucchini

2 tbsp fresh salsa

1 head fresh lettuce

cumin

smoked paprika

salt & pepper

DIRECTIONS

Sauté the filling:

1. In a skillet over medium heat, warm avocado oil. Add chopped zucchini and cook for 3-5 minutes, until tender. Stir in black beans, cumin, paprika, garlic powder, salt, and pepper. Cook for another 3–4 minutes until heated through.
2. Warm your tortillas:
3. Heat tortillas in a dry skillet until soft and warm, about 30 seconds per side.
4. Assemble:
5. Spoon the zucchini and bean mixture into each tortilla. Top with sliced avocado, a spoonful of salsa, fresh cilantro, lettuce, and a squeeze of lime.

Notes: We love cassava tortillas, crunchy Siete shells, or freshly made tortillas with spelt flour flour

Cosmic Comfort Stew

INGREDIENTS

2-4 cups bone broth
1 can full fat coconut milk
1.5 cup dry lentils, rinsed
4 carrots
3 celery stalks
1 head of cauliflower chopped
6 cloves of garlic
1 chunk fresh turmeric peeled and
finely chopped
1 small chunk fresh ginger peeled and
finely chopped
1 medium onion chopped
1 tsp salt season to taste
1/2 tsp coriander
1/2 tsp cumin
1/4 tsp curry powder
1/4 tsp curry powder
1/4 tsp turmeric powder
1 tbsp coconut oil

NOTES:

This is a family favorite. We
love making this on Sunday
as it makes many servings!
Pair with rice, gluten free
bread, or freshly made
tortillas.

DIRECTIONS

1. Sauté the aromatics: In a large pot, heat
   the coconut oil over medium heat. Add
   onion, garlic, fresh turmeric, and fresh
   ginger. Sauté for 3–4 minutes until frag
   and softened.
2. Add the veggies: Stir in the carrots, cele
   Cook for another 3–4 minutes, letting th
   veggies soak up the flavor.
3. Season: Sprinkle in the salt, coriander,
   cumin, curry powder, and ground
   turmeric. Stir well to coat the vegetable
   the spices.
4. Add lentils, cauliflower + liquids: Pour in
   the bone broth and coconut milk. Add th
   rinsed lentils. Stir everything together.
5. Simmer: Bring to a gentle boil, then redu
   the heat and let the stew simmer, cover
   for about 25–35 minutes, or until the ler
   are soft and the veggies are tender.
6. Taste + adjust: Taste your stew and adju
   seasoning as needed: more salt, a squee
   of lime, or extra curry powder if you like
   bolder flavor.
7. Serve: Ladle into bowls and enjoy warm.
   This stew pairs beautifully with sautéed
   greens or cabbage, avocado. Garnish wit
   cilantro and chopped cashews.

Tempeh Bánh Mi

INGREDIENTS:

For the tempeh marinade:
- 1 block tempeh, sliced into thin strips
- 2 tablespoons tamari or coconut aminos
- 1 tablespoon maple syrup
- 1 tablespoon rice vinegar or lime juice
- 1 teaspoon sesame oil
- 1 small clove garlic, minced
- 1/2 teaspoon grated ginger

For the quick pickles:
- 1 small carrot, julienned
- 4–5 radishes, thinly sliced
- 1/4 small red onion, thinly sliced
- 1/4 cup rice vinegar
- 1 tablespoon maple syrup or honey
- 1/4 teaspoon salt

Other:
- Cashew spread, vegan mayo, or avocado mayo
- Fresh cilantro
- Fresh cucumbers
- Gluten-free sourdough bread, sliced

DIRECTIONS:

- Marinate the tempeh: In a shallow dish, whisk together tamari, maple syrup, vinegar/lime, sesame oil, garlic, and ginger. Add the tempeh slices and coat well. Let marinate for at least 20 minutes (or longer for more flavor).
- Make the quick pickles:In a small bowl or jar, whisk rice vinegar, maple syrup, and salt. Add carrots, radish, and onion. Stir or shake to coat. Let sit while you prep everything else (at least 15 minutes).
- Cook the tempeh: Heat a little oil in a skillet over medium heat. Cook tempeh slices for 2–3 minutes per side until golden and caramelized.
- Assemble the sandwich: Spread cashew spread on each slice of gluten-free sourdough. Add tempeh, a generous amount of pickled veggies (drain excess liquid), fresh cucumbers, and fresh cilantro. Top with the second slice of bread.
- Enjoy! Slice in half and serve. You can add extra pickles or a squeeze of lime for brightness.

Cilantro Lime Coleslaw

INGREDIENTS

- 3 cups green or red cabbage finely shredded (use a mandolin for best texture
- 1 cup shredded carrots
- ¼ cup finely chopped red onion
- ¼ cup chopped fresh cilantro
- 2 tbsp chopped parsley
- Juice of 1–2 limes (to taste)
- 2 tbsp olive oil or avocado oil
- 1 tsp maple syrup or honey (optional)
- ½ tsp sea salt
- ¼ tsp black pepper
- Pinch of cumin or chili flakes (optional)

DIRECTIONS

1. In a large bowl, combine cabbage, carrots, onion, cilantro, and parsley.
2. In a small bowl, whisk together lime juice, oil, maple syrup (if using), salt, pepper, and any optional spices.
3. Pour the dressing over the veggies and toss until evenly coated.
4. Let sit for 10–15 minutes before serving to allow flavors to meld.

Tips:

1. This slaw is refreshing, light, and vibrant—perfect for bowls, tacos, or as a crunchy side. For creaminess, add a spoonful of your cashew crema or mashed avocado.

Almond Tuna

Ingredients

- 1 cup almonds (or cashew, pecan)
- 1 apple, chopped
- 2 celery stalks, chopped
- 2 pickles, chopped
- 2 green onions, chopped
- 1 sprig fresh dill, chopped
- 4 sprigs fresh parsley, chopped
- Juice of 1 lemon
- 3 tbsp vegan mayo (or substitute with olive oil)

Method

1. Instructions:
2. Mix all ingredients together and mix in a bowl until well combined.

Serving Ideas:

1. Enjoy with gluten-free crackers, on top gluten free sourdough bread or wrap in a Swiss chard leaf for a nourishing, high-vibe snack. Add more or less herbs & mayo per your preference.
2. Enjoy!

107

Sweet Potato Bites

Ingredients:

- 2 sweet potatoes soaked and sliced
- Coconut oil
- Cinnamon

Directions:

- Preheat oven to 375
- Cut the sweet potatoes into ¼ inch circles
- Toss with coconut oil and cinnamon
- Bake for 25-30 mins based on preference
- Less time for softer potatoes

Options:

- You can cut sweet potatoes into cute shapes to get children's attention

Nourishing Bowls

Cosmic Cobb

A kitchen sink kind of salad — when there's "nothing to eat," this bowl becomes everything

Ingredients

- 2-4 hard boiled eggs (I do hot start method, boil 10 mins, rinse with cool water)
- 1 head fresh lettuce, chopped
- meats of choice thinly sliced (I use turkey & pastrami)
- 2 tbsp hemp hearts
- 2 tbsp pumpkin seeds
- 1 shaved carrot
- 1 sliced cucumber
- golden glow citrus vinaigrette
- optional - avocado, tomato, cheese,

Directions

1. Prepare your base: Add the chopped greens to a large serving bowl or arrange them on a platter for that classic Cobb look.
2. Layer with intention: Neatly line up the toppings in rows — egg, carrot, meats, seeds — creating a rainbow of nourishment.
3. Dress & bless: Drizzle dressing over the top just before serving. Toss gently if you like or let each person mix their own.
4. Optional blessing: Pause, breathe in gratitude, and send love into your food before you nourish your body.

ROOT TO RISE BOWL

Ingredients

- ½ cup garbanzo beans
- 1 cup cilantro lime coleslaw
- ½ avocado
- 1 cup bone broth quinoa
- 1 tbsp cashew crema
- any additional toppings you like

Instructions:

1. Prep your ingredients ahead of time:
2. Cook the garbanzo beans (or use tetra pack, drained, and rinsed).
3. Cook the quinoa according to package directions and sub bone broth for water for extra nutrients
4. Make the coleslaw and crema
5. Assemble the bowl:
6. Add a scoop of quinoa to your bowl.
7. Top with garbanzo beans and coleslaw.
8. Add a spoonful of crema and half of an avocado (sliced or mashed).
9. Enjoy!
10. Perfect for lunch or dinner—fresh, filling, and full of flavor.

Recipes for garbanzo beans, crema, quinoa, and coleslaw included in book

Sauces & Dressings

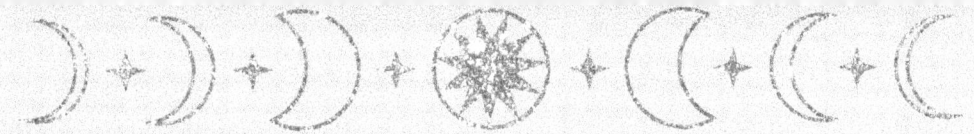

Cashew Crema

INGREDIENTS

1 cup cashews
1 cup water
¼ tsp salt
juice of 1/4-1/2 lemon

NOTES

We use this dip instead of
sour cream. We enjoy it on tacos,
burritos, buddha bowls,
and with chips.
To make it spicy, use this recipe and
add a chipotle pepper while blending.

DIRECTIONS

soak cashews in water for at least 30 mins.
pour cashews and water into blender
add salt and lemon or lime juice
blend for just under 1 min
store in glass jar for 10 days in fridge

Golden Glow Citrus Vinaigrette

INGREDIENTS

- 2 tablespoons fresh citrus juice (like lemon, lime, or orange — or a mix!)
- 1 teaspoon Dijon mustard
- 1 teaspoon honey (or more to taste)
- 2 tablespoons vinegar (apple cider vinegar or white wine vinegar work well)
- 1/4 teaspoon salt (or to taste)
- A few cracks of black pepper
- 1/4 cup olive oil

DIRECTIONS

1. In a small bowl or jar, whisk together the citrus juice, mustard, honey, vinegar, salt, and pepper until combined.
2. Slowly drizzle in the olive oil while whisking (or shake in a jar with a lid) until the dressing is smooth and creamy.
3. Taste and adjust — add a little more honey if you like it sweeter, or more citrus or vinegar for extra tang.
4. Keep in fridge, remove 30 mins prior to use.

Star Snacks & Soul Treats

Cosmic Crunch
Conscious crunch. Pure nourishment.

SERVINGS: 2   PREPPING TIME: 10 MIN   COOKING TIME: 16 MINS

INGREDIENTS

2 cups oats

½ cup pecans

½ cup almonds

3-5 tbsp honey

3-5 tbsp coconut oil

1 tbsp maca powder

¼ cup pumpkin seeds

1 tbsp chia seeds

1 tbsp cocoa powder

1-2 pinch sea salt

2 tbsp nut butter
(optional for richer
flavor)

DIRECTIONS

1. Preheat oven to 325
2. Mix oats, chopped nuts, pumpkin seeds, maca, cocoa powder, chia seeds and salt
3. Melt coconut oil
4. Mix in honey and nut butter with coconut oil
5. Mix liquid into dry ingredients
6. Mix well
7. Cover baking sheet with parchment paper and flatten wet mixture with spatula
8. Cook for 8 mins
9. Rotate cooking sheet and cook for 8 more mins
10. Remove from oven and let granola set for at least 20 mins... if you can 🤭
11. Store in glass jar and enjoy within a week

I highly recommend high quality organic oats. Conventional oats are among the most pesticide-contaminated crops.. Eats well alone, with nut or seed milk, or coconut yogurt.

PINEAPPLE
HERB
SMOOTHIE

Ingredients:

1 cup chopped fresh pineapple
1 cup mixed herbs (cilantro, mint, basil, parsley)
1 cup coconut milk

Directions:

Mix all ingredients in blender for 1 minute
Pour in cup with ice
Enjoy!

COSMIC COCOA PUDDING

Instructions

- Scoop and Blend
- Scoop the avocado into a blender or food processor.
- Add Ingredients: Add cocoa powder, maple syrup, coconut milk, vanilla, and salt.
- Blend Until Smooth: Blend everything until silky smooth and creamy. Scrape down the sides if needed.
- Taste and Adjust
- Taste it—add a little more maple syrup if you want it sweeter.
- Chill (Optional)
- You can eat it right away or chill it in the fridge for 30 minutes for a firmer texture.
- Serve
- Spoon into bowls or jars. Top with fresh fruit and enjoy!

Ingredients

- 2 large ripe avocados
- ½ unsweetened cocoa powder
- ½ maple syrup
- ½ cup full fat coconut milk
- 1 tsp vanillq
- 1 pinch salt
- fresh fruit

Thank you for going on this journey with me.

This book was born from a moment of deep inspiration during a meditation in my Dragon Consciousness Program. While traveling among the stars, we were blessed by a group of Starseeds who shared messages of hope for humanity. I was given the chance to ask a question—and in return, I received two beautiful messages for my two beautiful children.
In that moment, I realized I had been preparing for some time to write this book.
My prayer is that you connect with yourself, with your soul, and remember your true nature on Earth. We are source consciousness having a human experience—and my hope is that something within these pages has touched, inspired, or helped you reclaim a sacred part of who you truly are.

In gratitude, in light, and in love—
Chelsea

A personal note from me:

Follow me on Instagram @knowbysoul

I started Know by Soul over two years ago when I first began baking gluten-free sourdough—and I'm happy to say, my starter is officially mature!

These days, you'll find me in the kitchen baking, out on a hike, studying astrology, playing games with my family, binging a show on Netflix when I need a break, or dreaming up our next big adventure.

Alongside my beautiful and talented friend @tiffanyvillegiante, we host monthly Sacred Sister Ceremonies and biannual spiritual retreats that bring women together in remembrance, healing, and joy.

Stay tuned for where Spirit leads us next..

Clean Living Resources & Inspirations:

When I choose products for our home and bodies, I do my best to pick what's safe, gentle, and supportive of our energy. I check EWG (Environmental Working Group) ratings and — most importantly — I trust my intuition. If something doesn't feel right, I listen.

Here are some of the products, materials, and ideas that work for us:

🔍 Kitchen & Cooking

- Cast iron pans — durable, naturally nonstick with seasoning
- Stainless steel pans — safe for high heat cooking
- Ceramic-coated pans — easy to clean, non-toxic
- Glassware for leftovers — no plastic leaching
- Ghee — perfect for high-heat cooking
- Coconut oil — great for high heat, naturally antimicrobial
- Olive oil — best for salads, drizzling, and low-heat cooking
- Seventh Generation dishwasher pods — plant-based, no phosphates or chlorine
- ECOS dishwashing soap — biodegradable, no synthetic fragrance
- Ecover rinse aid — eco-friendly, works well

🧺 Laundry & Cleaning

- Aspen Clean laundry pods — minimal ingredients, plant- and mineral-based
- Attitude unscented laundry soap — hypoallergenic, gentle
- Dr. Bronner's soap — multi-purpose and natural

Home Goods
- Organic cotton or linen bedding and towels
- Non-toxic paint — ECOS, Clare
- Beeswax or coconut wax candles — cleaner burn than paraffin, scented with essential oil, not fragrance
- Air-purifying plants — like snake plant, peace lily
- Essential oil diffusers + pure essential oils

For the Kiddos
- Everyone products — gentle, plant-based
- Griffin bath bubbles and lotions — fun and clean
- Tallow balm — nourishing, minimal
- Glass, silicone, stainless snack containers — safe storage without plastic

Body & Personal Care
- Everyone hand soap — EWG-verified, essential oil scented
- Tallow body products — choose those scented with essential oils, not fragrance
- Mineral-based sunscreens — Badger, Babo Botanicals, Thinksport, Attitude
- Natural deodorants — Native (unscented), Tallow based
- Fluoride-free toothpaste — Attitude, Toms, Desert Essence
- Organic cotton pads- The Honey Pot

Lifestyle & Wellness
- Beeswax wraps — reusable alternative to plastic wrap
- Water filtration systems — lifesource, reverse osmosis, Kangen water

- Mindful tech practices —unplug WIFI at night, grounding mat
- Shopping local — farmer's market, organic co-op

Resources & Inspirations

If you feel called to explore these ideas further, here are some of the teachings, tools, and books that have inspired my journey:

Joe Dispenza
Books & teachings on creating your reality, meditation, and the science of transformation.
— Breaking the Habit of Being Yourself

Nikola Tesla & the 369 Code
The inspiration behind the 369 manifestation method, rooted in Tesla's belief in the power of numbers and universal energy.

The Law of Attraction
There are countless books and teachers on this topic.
— Ask and It Is Given by Esther and Jerry Hicks

Journey of The Soul by Cynthia Brown

Bringers of the Dawn by Barbara Marciniak
A powerful channeled book that reminds us of our Starseed origins and purpose during this great time of awakening.

The Three Waves of Volunteers & The New Earth by Dolores Cannon

Mantra & Sacred Sound

For those interested in exploring mantras and the power of the voice, I recommend looking into:

- Snatam Kaur (music)
- Siri Sadhana Kaur
- Hansu Jot
- White Sun

Consciousness Program - Ascension Wisdom Institute

Join Carla Macapinlac on the journey of Healing, Learning, and Expansion.

The Mahanraj's - Great Divine Flow Yoga

Online and in-person Kundalini yoga classes that support deep nervous system healing, spiritual awakening, and connection to your inner divine.

www.ingramcontent.com/pod-product-compliance
Lightning Source LLC
Chambersburg PA
CBHW041537120626
46551CB00019B/2737